Working Children

[1] Sheelin' mussels, Auchmithie, c.1895.

Working Children

An Illustrated Account of Child Employment in Scotland in the Nineteenth Century

Derek Ogston and Margaret Carlaw

BAILLIEKNOWE PUBLISHING

Baillieknowe Publishing
Baillieknowe
Stichill, Kelso
TD5 7TB

First Published 2003

British Library Cataloguing in Publication Data

A catalogue record for this book is available from the British Library

ISBN 0-9538590-2-9

Printed by Kelso Graphics, Kelso

Acknowledgements

Help in the production of this small book came from a number of sources. We are particularly grateful to Jim and Margaret Carruthers of St Andrews Fine Art and Duane Mead of the Rendez-Vous Gallery, Aberdeen for allowing us to photograph paintings in their galleries, and to Sotheby's, Bond Street, London for providing images of a number of paintings. Our thanks are also due to Helen McPherson for the photography of paintings in private collections. We acknowledge the assistance and cooperation of staff of the Scottish Life Archive of the National Museums of Scotland, and a number of other museums and libraries who permitted us to use photographs for which they hold copyright, and we are indebted to the National Galleries of Scotland, Aberdeen Art Gallery, Dundee Art Gallery and the Hunterian Art Gallery for their help. The comments on an early manuscript and the advice of William Burnett were invaluable.

Derek Ogston
Margaret Carlaw

November 2003

Contents

[2] View of New Lanark.
Watercolour by John Winning, c.1818.

Introduction

The industrial revolution began in Britain in the eighteenth century and was to alter radically the working patterns over much of the country, including large parts of Scotland, with profound effects on the lives of many children. The changes that took place encompassed the utilisation of more efficient sources of power, in particular, steam power fuelled by coal; the development of machines for the large-scale production of goods to satisfy expanding populations at home and abroad; and the concentration of production into large factories and mills. From a predominantly rural nation Britain became an urban one with the migration of large numbers from the countryside to the rapidly growing towns and cities where most of the factories were sited. Poverty was rife with many families at or below subsistence levels. Life expectancy in the working classes was short and infant and child mortality was high.

Children in the industrial areas of Scotland were employed in the factories, mills and mines, exploited by owners at very low wages, while parents were forced to send their children to such work for the small supplement brought to the family income and essential for survival. The result was that large numbers of children, many of tender years, worked long hours, often in grim and unhealthy environments. Others, unable to find work, resorted to eking out a precarious living in the streets of the cities through begging, stealing or occasional menial tasks.

In the rural areas children had long been expected to assist the crofter or farmer or to contribute to the work of the fishing families in the costal areas. Such employment of children for a wage or to labour for their own families continued in the nineteenth century, but often to the detriment of their education. The limited or lack of formal education resulted in considerable illiteracy.

Throughout the nineteenth century there were endeavours by a number of philanthropists to improve the lot of working children, either by personal initiatives or by campaigning for legislation to end the worst of the abuses. Through a series of Parliamentary Acts the lives of many children were improved by laws forbidding their employment in a number of particularly harsh and dangerous occupations and by progressively raising the age at which they could be employed in other types of work. Such measures did not cover all occupations and large numbers of children continued to labour in unfavourable conditions until the later decades of the century when, under the provisions of the Education Act of 1872, schooling became compulsory for all between the ages of five and thirteen years, later raised to fourteen. Even after this time, however, many children took jobs before or after school hours to bolster the family income or to provide pocket money.

The range of work undertaken by children over the nineteenth century in Scotland as recorded in written archive and, later in the century, in photographs, has been surveyed in this text. Additionally, the visual representation of children at work in drawings and paintings by artists of the time, including the illustrators of books and periodicals, has been examined. It was hoped that the visual records would supplement the written accounts and add to our knowledge of social conditions as they affected children in the Victorian era.

Working practices did not alter abruptly at the turn of either the eighteenth or nineteenth century. While the text and images describe and illustrate those of the nineteenth century this period has been interpreted broadly with, where appropriate, extension into the preceding or succeeding centuries. Similarly, while the illustrations are predominantly of Scottish settings, a few depict English situations where these are indistinguishable from equivalent Scottish scenes.

Chapter 1

Legislation Governing the Employment of Children

The initial movements aimed at regulating child labour in Great Britain began in the latter years of the eighteenth century, a time when the rapid growth of manufacturing had resulted in the exploitation of young children in mining and industrial work. Throughout the nineteenth century a reduction in the prevalence and harshness of child labour was achieved by piecemeal legislation that raised the minimum age at which employment was permitted, excluded children from some particularly harmful working environments, limited the hours worked per day and made employment conditional on part-time attendance at school or evidence of some educational attainment.

The first Acts were concerned with the plight of chimney sweepers' boys, those children who from the age of five years were compelled to climb chimneys in order to clean or extinguish fires in them. In the *Act for the Better Regulation of Chimney Sweepers and the Apprentices* of 1788 a minimum age for the employment of climbing boys was fixed at eight. In 1834, under the *Chimney Sweep Act*, the binding of any boy under ten was forbidden, and employment of children under fourteen not allowed unless apprenticed or on trial; boys were to have a two month trial before being apprenticed with examination by a magistrate at the end of that time and not to be bound unless willing. Mainly as a result of the efforts of Lord Shaftesbury, a Bill was passed in 1840 prohibiting the employment of any person under the age of twenty-one to climb chimneys and forbidding anyone under the age of sixteen to be apprenticed to a chimney sweep (*Act for Regulation of Chimney Sweeps and Chimneys*).

The *Mines and Collieries Act* of 1842 forbade the employment of boys under ten and girls of any age below ground. In a second Act of 1860 the minimum age for boys working below ground rose to twelve. It allowed, however, boys of ten and eleven to be employed if they were either attending school twice a week or could produce an educational certificate showing that they had some proficiency in reading, writing and arithmetic. The minimum age for boys working below ground was raised to twelve in 1872 and to thirteen in 1900.

Early legislation relating to the textile factories and applying principally to pauper apprentices was the *Health and Morals of Apprentices Act* of 1802. It was intended to abolish night work and to limit the working day in cotton and woollen mills to twelve hours, work not to commence before 6 a.m. Also in the Act were regulations concerning proper clothing; every apprentice was to be supplied with two complete suits of clothing, stockings, hats and shoes. Male and female apprentices had to be provided with separate sleeping apartments and not more than two were to sleep in one bed. The Act also contained provision for instruction in reading, writing and arithmetic in each working day and religious instruction on Sundays. Some attempt to improve the conditions in the factories was made by the stipulation that all rooms were to be lime-washed twice a year and duly ventilated. The *Cotton Mills and Factories Act* of 1819 made nine years the minimum age for employment in cotton mills, and restricted those over the age of nine to a twelve hour day. Both these early attempts to curb child labour in the cotton mills were, however, largely ineffectual because of the absence of an independent inspectorate to ensure that factory owners abided by the regulations.

The *Mills and Factory Act* of 1833 laid down a minimum age of nine years for the employment of children in all textile mills, and limited their working time to eight hours in the day up to the age of thirteen. Employment during the night hours of 8.30 p.m. and 5.30 a.m. was prohibited. Children working in factories had to obtain a certificate of age from local doctors, but there is evidence that the age limits were frequently abused. Importantly, provision was made in the Act for the appointment of four factory inspectors.

In 1844 the *Labour and Factory Act* reduced the hours of work for children between the ages of eight and thirteen years in textile factories to six and a half a day, either in the morning or afternoon. Certificates of age were to be granted only by appointed surgeons, and certificates of school attendance obtained. For the first time there was a requirement for machinery to be guarded. The maximum hours of work permitted for children were reduced to ten per day and 58 in any one week in an Act passed in 1847 (*Hours of Labour of Young Persons and Females in Factories Act*). In 1874 the minimum age for work in all textile factories including lace was set at nine years, raised to ten in 1875, with the minimum age for full time work being set at fourteen, or thirteen conditional on production of an educational certificate.

Acts covering non-textile factories and workshops began to appear in 1845 when a minimum age of eight for work in print works was laid down (*Calico Print Works Act*). The same age limit was set for bleach and dye works in 1860 (*Bleach and Dye Works Act*), and for earthenware, match, percussion caps and cartridges, paper staining and fustian cutting factories in 1864. All non-textile factories and workshops were covered by the 1867 *Workshops Regulation Act* with eight years being set as the minimum age for employment. In 1878 all factories and workshops were included in an Act making ten the minimum age for working; in the *Factory and Workshop Act* of 1891 the minimum age was raised to eleven years, the age of fourteen being retained for full-time work, thirteen if an educational certificate was held.

Special provisions of the Factories Acts established higher minimum ages for employment in dangerous occupations. The *Factory Acts Extension Act* of 1867, for example, established a minimum age of eleven for the metal grinding trades, sixteen for girls in brickmaking and twelve for boys in melting and annealing glass.

Legislation on one of the abuses of children working on the land came with the *Agricultural Gangs Act* of 1867 which prohibited the employment of children under the age of eight years in public agricultural gangs and required gangmasters to be licensed. The general employment of children in agriculture was addressed in the *Agricultural Children's Act* of 1873: it stipulated that children between the ages of eight and ten years could only be employed if a certificate stating that 250 school attendances had been made was signed by the parent. For children over ten years 150 attendances over the preceding 12 months were required.

An attempt to regulate the hours of work of children and young persons in shops was made through the *Shop Hours Regulation Act* of 1886 which limited work to 74 hours per week.

Overall the legislation enacted by the Parliamentary Acts during the nineteenth century, both those quoted above and others, progressively placed controls on the most serious abuses of children working in mines, factories, shops and agriculture and in such specific occupations as chimney sweeping. While child labour was not abolished, limitations on the age of starting work, the hours of work and exposure to hazards had been achieved.

Chapter 2

Employment in Industrial and Urban Areas

The effect of the Parliamentary Acts limiting the age and hours worked was to eliminate many of the abuses of child labour around the middle decades of the nineteenth century. The Mines and Factory Acts, however, did not encompass all types of employment and young children continued to work long hours for paltry wages in many occupations. The Acts of the 1830s and 1840s made it an offence to employ children under the age of nine years, but some employers were tempted to evade the law. Where the presentation of certificates of educational attainment was required for employment, these could be purchased from unscrupulous teachers:

> The teachers in both schools stated that they were frequently applied to for certificates to children who intended to apply for admission to printfields, etc., who had either not been at school at all, or for a sufficient length of time. One of them said, "He had been offered 6d. or 1s. for such certificate"; but usually the inquiry was "What he charged?"[1]

The census returns for 1861 recording occupations according to age-group revealed 950 boys and 698 girls under the age of ten years in work. The most frequent occupations recorded for boys were *Tobacco, Cigar and Snuff Manufacturing* (89), *Cattleman* (86), *Calico, Cotton, Printer* (75), *Cotton Manufacture* (65), *Messenger, Porter, Errand Boy* (65), *Factory Labourer* (59) and *Flax, Linen Manufacture* (48). Girls' occupations were *Domestic Servants* (173), *Cotton Manufacture* (107), *Calico, Cotton, Printer* (95), *Factory Labourer* (95) and *Flax, Linen Manufacture* (71).[2] The numbers employed in the same age-group in the 1871 census returns fell to 299 boys and 324 girls.[3]

Coal Mines

Up to the passage of the Mines and Colleries Act of 1842 the coal mines of Scotland employed large numbers of children in the earlier decades of the nineteenth century. The *Report of the Children's Employment Commission (Mines)*, published in 1842, provided many details on the conditions of work in the British mines including those in Scotland.[4] It included verbatim statements from child workers, mine proprietors and managers, many testifying to the harshness of the life, the dangers and the deleterious effects on the health of the children.

Coal fields were widely distributed throughout central Scotland including East Lothian, Midlothian, West Lothian, Stirlingshire, Dumbartonshire,

Clackmannanshire, Fifeshire, Lanarkshire, Ayrshire and Renfrewshire. It was common practice in the collieries in the east of Scotland for children to begin working at the age of seven or eight, and some even started at five or six years of age. Less commonly, enlightened proprietors and managers kept children under the age of ten or twelve out of their pits. In the west of Scotland eight years was the usual age of beginning work in the mines.

Children in the east of Scotland were employed in trapping, coal-bearing, putting, pumping and hewing. Trapping consisted of opening and shutting a door to allow the coal wagons to pass and required the child to sit in the dark for long periods, often many hours.

Coal-bearing was particularly hard work, almost always carried out by girls or women, rarely by boys. It involved carrying coal in baskets on their backs with burdens varying from three-quarters to three hundredweight from the coal-face to the pit-bottom and frequently required climbing a number of ladders [3]. Injury from falling off the ladders, or from loads dropping on those below was not uncommon. A typical statement given to the Commissioners is that from a twelve-year old girl:

> I am wrought with sister and brother; it is very sore work. Cannot say how many rakes or journeys I make from pit-bottom to wall-face and back, thinks about 30 or 25 on the average; distance varies from 100 to 250 fathoms. I carry a hundredweight and a quarter on my back, and am frequently in water up to the calves of my legs. When first down fell frequently asleep while waiting for coal from heat and fatique. I do not like the work, nor do the lassies, but they are made to like it. When the weather is warm there is difficulty in breathing, and frequently the lights go out.

[3] Girls coal-bearing on ladder.

Dragging or pushing carts containing coal from the coal-wall to the pit-bottom was known as coal-putting. The carts used to carry loads varying from three to ten hundredweight were either the 'hutchie', an oblong square-sided box with four wheels and usually run on a rail [4], or the 'slype', a wood-framed box curved and shod with iron at the bottom [5]. Where the roofs were low the carriages had to be dragged with the children on hands and knees.

[4] Putting using the 'hutchie'.

[5] Putting using the 'slype'.

A number of the pits required constant pumping of water to prevent flooding. This was a particularly strenuous job allowing no time to rest and often necessitating standing in water. Children were also required to carry the water away in buckets.

Some boys from nine years of age and upwards were employed in hewing at the coal-face in mines in the east of Scotland, but this was unusually young for such work and peculiar to the district.

In the west of Scotland girls and women were much less frequently employed and none were engaged in coal-bearing. Apart from trapping, the principal work for children in these areas was drawing or pushing a loaded 'whirley' that ran on cast-iron wheels along the tram-roads from where the coal was worked to the bottom of the shaft; here it was hoisted up with its load. Up to the age of fourteen years children usually drew in pairs, one pulling and the other pushing from behind.

Although there is a paucity of pictorial material from the early nineteenth century of children in Scottish mines, the *Report of the Children's Employment Commission (Mines)* of 1842 is illustrated with a notable series of drawings. These are considered to have been of particular value both in alerting the public to the hazards of injury and ill-health to children working in the mines and in influencing opinion in favour of legislative action. The risk of immorality implied by some of the drawings was of particular concern to many people.

Ironstone Mines and Manufacture of Iron

In the east of Scotland young boys and girls were sent down into the ironstone pits to carry out work similar to that of the coal mines.[5] Children were employed in the ironstone works of the west of Scotland from around nine years of age, but drawing was too heavy for children and not performed by them.[6]

Employment in the iron works involved the making of coke, the calcining of ironstone, the blasting in the furnace and the casting of iron. The refining of iron, the changing of crude iron into wrought iron by puddling, a process invented in 1784, involved drawing hot gases over a charge of pig iron and iron ore held on the furnace hearth. The product was stirred and as loss of carbon took place it was worked into balls which were subsequently forged and finally passed through the rolling mills.

Children were employed to build up piles of coal to be converted into coke in the field adjoining the furnaces, to build heaps of ironstone and coal in preparation for the process of calcination, and to break the limestone into small pieces before it was thrown into the blast furnaces. Some were employed in the immediate attendance on the blast furnace, filling boxes or barrows with coke, coal, calcined ironstone or broken limestone.[7]

Lead Mines

In the Leadhills and Wanlockhead area of the Lowther Hills lead was mined: boys were employed to assist in the washing of the lead ore. They usually started work at the age of nine or ten, sometimes as young as eight, and the regular working day was ten hours, but extra time had frequently to be worked. The labour involved constant contact with cold water and exposure to adverse weather.[8] Boys around the age of twelve were used in the mines to haul out the ore (galena) on troughs. The mortality of children in these areas was high, due in part to the working conditions and to the air and water pollution arising from the lead.

Textile Industry

The textile industry employed large numbers of children in the nineteenth century. The industry covered the production of yarns and fabrics and included the process of spinning in the production of yarn, weaving yarn into fabric, and knitting. Embroidery, lace-making and the manufacture of cord, rope and nets were also components of the industry. The natural fibres available in the eighteenth and nineteenth centuries were cotton, wool, jute, flax and silk. Silk does not require to be spun, but other fibres require drawing out and twisting together to join them firmly in a continuous yarn.

The minutes of evidence given to the *Committee on the Bill to Regulate the Labour of Children in the Mills and Factories of the United Kingdom* in 1832 reveal the widespread exploitation and maltreatment of many young children in the textile industry in the late eighteenth and early nineteenth centuries. The children, often starting work at the age of seven years or even younger, worked up to fourteen or fifteen hours a day in unhealthy and uncomfortable environments. In addition to the dusty atmosphere the temperature in the mills was frequently maintained at around 85° F, the heat necessary to make the cotton fibres open or draw. The children were usually required to be on their feet for the great majority of the time and the distance covered in the mill for many was estimated at eight to ten miles over the working day. Many reports referred to the pale, emaciated and stunted children, some with limb deformities attributable to their posture at work. Fatigue and drowsiness were almost constant after many hours at work, occasioning accidents and cruel beatings to keep the children awake. Many of the children were orphans from poorhouses: a number in the Dundee mills came from Edinburgh or Perth. They were apprenticed for from two to five years, and kept locked up night and day to prevent them leaving. Those trying to escape were severely thrashed when caught.[9] The following is a passage from an account of a boy sent to work in a Dundee spinning mill:

> The lash of the slave driver was never more unsparingly used in Carolina on the unfortunate slaves than the canes and 'whangs' of mill foremen were then used on helpless factory boys. When I went to a spinning mill I was about seven years of age. I had to get out of bed every morning at five o'clock, commence work at half-past five, drop at nine for breakfast, begin again at half-past nine, work until two, which was the dinner hour, start again at half-past two, and continue until half-past seven at night. Such were the nominal hours; but in reality there were no regular hours; masters and managers did with us as they liked. The clocks at the factories were often put forward in the morning and back at night, and instead of being instruments for the measurement of time, they were used as *cloaks* for cheatery and oppression. Though this was known amongst the hands, all were afraid to speak, and a workman then was afraid to carry a watch, as it was no uncommon event to dismiss any one who presumed to know too much about the science of horology.

> It was during this winter that I got the first unmerciful beating from a mill overseer. I was attending a spinning frame. It got too full in the shifting, and I was unable to keep up the ends. The foreman challenged me. I told him I was doing the best I could. He flew into a furious passion, dragged me into the

turning shop, cut a strap off a lathe, and lashed me cruelly. He
then seized me by the ears and hung me for a few moments
over a window three storeys from the ground.[10]

The plight of children working in the factories was not a subject that attracted
the attention of artists in oil or watercolour. Reproductions of woodcuts,
etchings and engravings of children in employment in industry were used,
however, to illustrate periodicals and literary works. The accuracy of
representation ranged widely, dependent on the purposes of the image. While
some were descriptive of the scenes portrayed, others were caricatures or satirical
cartoons intended to sway public opinion or further political aims. Their value
as a historical record of the life of children employed in mines and factories at
the time is, accordingly, variable.

The concerns of social reformers including a number of politicians over the
exploitation of children in the textile industry in the earlier decades of the
nineteenth century resulted in a variety of types of image. Cartoons, such as
those drawn by Robert Cruickshank [6], gave a clear message of child abuse in
the cotton mills to the public. The novels of some writers included illustrations,
often by well-known and talented artists, of working children. Frances Trollop
(1780-1863) became involved in the campaign against child employment in
factories. Her book *Michael Armstrong: Factory Boy*, which was published in
parts, the first appearing in 1840, contained a number of plates by a French
artist, Augustre Hervieu, who had accompanied Trollop to Manchester to visit
factories. Illustrations in this volume include scenes of piecers and scavengers at

[6] "How children suffered in factories".
Illustration by Robert Cruickshank, 1832.

21

[7] "Love conquered fear".
Illustration by Augustre Hervieu for *Michael Armstrong: Factory Boy* by Frances Trollop, London, 1840.

[8] "Make haste, young un' or they wont leave a turnip paring for us".
Illustration by Augustre Hervieu for *Michael Armstrong: Factory Boy* by Frances Trollop, London, 1840.

[9] "A serious gentleman as owns a factory".
Illustration by Augustre Hervieu for *Michael Armstrong: Factory Boy* by Frances Trollop, London, 1840.

work in a textile factory as a background to the meeting of the two young brothers [7], of mill children competing for food at a pig trough [8], and of weary children waiting outside a Sabbath school [9].

Cotton Manufacture

The requirement by the weavers for greater quantities of yarn than traditional methods of spinning could provide led to the development of water-powered cotton mills with a large work force. The first of these in Scotland was operating by 1778 and by 1814 there were 120, mainly in Lanarkshire and Renfrewshire and mostly small in size. The largest was the New Lanark mill on the Clyde founded by David Dale and later to be owned by his son-in-law Robert Owen (1771–1858) who had previously managed a large spinning factory in Manchester.

The effects of the conditions under which children were forced to work in the cotton industry were recognized early. In the *Statistical Account of Scotland* relating to the Abbey Parish of Paisley and dating from the late eighteenth century the following passage is included:

> It is painful to think, that a manufacture which gives employment to so many hands, and which may be the source of great wealth to individuals, may be productive of very unhappy effects upon both the health and morals of the children employed in it. This there is some reason to apprehend. The numbers that are brought together, especially in the larger mills, the confinement, the breathing of an air laden with the dust and downy particles of the cotton, and contaminated with the effluvia of rancid oil rising from the machinery, must prove hurtful, in a high degree, to the delicate and tender lungs of children. Add to this, that mills which produce the water-twist are kept going day and night; and children must be had who are willing to work through the night, and sleep during the day. Tempted by the wages, parents send their children to this employment at a very early age, when they have got little or no education; and the close confinement deprives them of the opportunity of acquiring more. Ignorance, disease, and mortality, are but too likely to prove the effects of this manufacture, if carried on by unfeeling and selfish men. The characters of the gentlemen engaged in it in this neighbourhood give reason to hope, that every method will be employed which humanity and good sense can suggest to prevent these evils.[11]

Robert Owen was born at Newtown, a small market town in Montgomeryshire. At the age of ten he became an apprentice to a retail linen and wool draper in

Lincolnshire: he had subsequent apprenticeships in London and Manchester. By the age of 19 he was the superintendent of a large cotton mill in Manchester, later becoming manager and partner in the firm. He then persuaded his partners to purchase the New Lanark mills.

Owen's concern for the working children in the mills at the time led him to reduce the working day to 12 hours and not to employ children younger than ten years of age. He opposed physical punishment in factories and banned its use in the New Lanark mills. Owen believed that education was the key to the development of good character and the qualities that he wanted in his workers, and in 1816 he built a school in the New Lanark village. This school, which was attended by the younger children, became the first infant school in Britain.

[10] Statue of Robert Owen, Newtown, Powys.

Older children working in the mill also had to attend school for part of the day. The fame of the mills and village at New Lanark resulted in a number of paintings and engravings of the buildings [2]. Robert Owen is commemorated for his pioneering work by a statue in Newtown [10].

In 1815 Robert Owen sent proposals to Parliament for factory reform and the improvement in the conditions of children in mills, but the Parliamentary bill that ensued was much reduced in rigour and the resulting Factory Act of 1819 applied only to cotton mills. It did, however, prohibit the employment of children less than nine years of age and restricted the period of work of those under sixteen to twelve hours a day.

Steam power was later applied to spinning machinery, but the machinery was expensive and return on the capital outlay required day and night working, leading to men, women and children tending the machines for long periods. Very young children, known as 'scavengers' often worked between the spinners' feet, shifting bobbins and removing fluff from the spinning frames; small children were employed to do this as they were able to squeeze under the machines for cleaning while they were still operating, making it a dangerous job. Other young children worked as 'piecers' who had to lean over the spinning machines to repair broken threads.

Spinning machinery was progressively improved, providing finer quality yarn with less labour. One machine, called the 'mule', was invented by Samuel Crompton at the end of the 1770s and combined the principles of Richard Arkwright's water-frame and James Hargreaves' spinning jenny. With the mule the manual aid of a spinner was unnecessary, but children were still required to join the broken threads [11].

[11] Scavengers and piecers at work.
From *The History of Cotton Manufacture* by Edward Baines, London, 1835.

25

Later in the century, when the worst abuses of child labour in the textile industry had been abolished by the Factory Acts, illustrations of workers in the factories often included children, but gave a less harrowing picture of life in such employment. The appearances generally matched those seen in photographs of the time [12].

[12] Jute workers, Dundee, c.1900.

Linen Production

Flax required to be broken down as an initial step in the production of linen yarn and fabric. This was achieved by beating and scouring in water-powered mills, followed by combing, straightening, separating and splitting the fibres by drawing them through teeth, a process termed heckling. With the introduction of steam power the teeth of the heckle were attached to turning rollers and the flax fed into them. This latter task was often undertaken by children.

The *New Statistical Account of Scotland* includes the following:

> At present (1832) there are upwards of thirty flax spinning-mills in Dundee and the immediate neighbourhood, driven by a steam power........ In these mills about 3000 persons are daily employed. Of these there are under 18 years of age 1073 individuals; under 14 600; some under 12, and even from six to seven years of age.[12]

Processing of Jute

Many of the flax mills of Dundee switched to the processing of jute in the 1840s and 1850s and by the end of the nineteenth century Dundee was the major supplier of the world's requirements for jute products. The textile mills of Dundee, both flax and jute, employed large numbers of children who worked long hours for very low wages. Small children of a young age worked as 'pickers' removing the dust that had collected on the underside of the machinery.

Silk Manufacture

The raw material for the manufacture of silk was imported to Britain from Asia and the south of Europe, but the heavy import duty imposed up to 1824 curtailed development of the industry. On its reduction there was a large increase in the number of mills in England engaged in the twisting of silk threads. The weaving of silk was also carried out in Paisley and in other areas in Scotland. As in other parts of the textile industry children were widely employed and references to such work are found in the parish returns of the *New Statistical Account of Scotland*, for example:

> At a short distance from that village, a factory for throwing silk was erected in 1824. The number of persons employed in this factory averages 250. Of these, the larger proportion are children, none of whom are under eight years of age. The grown up people are at work eleven hours a-day, and the children for ten to eleven hours.[13]

Woollen Goods Manufacture

The historic technique of spinning, distaff spinning, improved by the introduction of the spinning wheel, remained in use in cottages in Scotland up to recent times. Many country children learned the skill [13], and it was a subject for artistic depiction [14].

[13] Spinners, Scotland, 1895.

[14] Hugh Cameron, *The Spinning Lesson*.

Between 1780 and 1830 the Borders emerged as the main area of wool-manufacturing in Scotland. Until the 1830s hosiery-making with the manufacture of stockings and woollen underwear was the principal industry. Thereafter the plaid became popular, later tartan cloths became fashionable, and the term 'tweed' was given to checked woollen products. Knitted goods continued to be made in the Borders throughout the century [15].

[15] Hand knitting machine, Hawick, 1889.

Technical innovations assisted in the growth of the Scottish woollen industry. There were improvements in the carding machines used to disentangle the wool and the process of spinning was made more continuous. One problem had been the necessity of taking the wool slivers from the carders and hand feeding them on to a machine for rough spinning before spinning the final yarn. Small children often carried out the hard task of hand feeding, but in the 1830s a 'piecing' machine was made in Hawick that dispensed with the need for child piecers.

Weaving

Hand-loom weaving was gradually replaced by the power loom and mechanical cotton weaving was introduced sometime after 1825 with linen weaving following some years later. As a result of mechanisation most hand-loom weavers went out of business and had to find employment in factories. Pockets of hand-loom weaving did survive as this technique could produce the high quality customised goods sometimes required.

The draw-loom was more complicated than the ordinary handloom, and each weaver required the assistance of a draw-boy who had to pull different bundles of cords on the command of the weaver to control the pattern. An engraving depicting handloom weaving and including a draw-boy from *Reminiscences of Eighty Years* by John Urie, the son of a Paisley weaver and himself a draw-boy for a short time, is illustrated [16]. Reference is made to draw-boy weaving in the *Report of the Children's Employment Commission* of 1843:

> In Glasgow, Paisley, and the neighbourhood, they also begin as early as six years of age; but at Kilmarnock and the vicinity, "the work being heavy, the drawers, who are all boys, do not commence it before twelve years of age: some looms, however, are worked by treading, in place of drawing, and in these the boys begin about ten years old".[14]

[16] Handloom weaving and draw-boy.
Engraving by W. Barr for
Reminiscences of Eighty Years
by John Urie, London, 1908.

Calico Printing

Calico is a cotton fabric: much was bleached, dyed and printed with one or more colours, and used for clothing and household purposes. Comments on children employed in this work include:

> In the East of Scotland children commence work at the same early ages. The Rev. John Dempster, minister of Denny, county of Stirling, states that in that parish, from the temptation of wages for their children, infants may be seen at work as early as five years of age; that "not a few are sent to work at five years old, with having got at school little more than a knowledge of the alphabet; and that they go to continuous employment at all ages from seven upwards".[15]

> About seven-eighths of the population inhabit the Vale of Leven, and are employed at the public works, bleachfields and printfields: to these works the children are sent, in too many cases, at and under seven years of age; and any learning they get afterwards is at the week day evening and Sunday evening schools.[16]

Embroidery

An occupation, particularly common in Ayrshire, was the embroidery of muslin to make into such articles as gowns and collars. A number of firms stamped patterns on muslin which was distributed to private houses where the embroidery was carried out. In Kilmarnock there were some sewing schools where children either received instruction in sewing in return for working for the mistress or paid for the teaching and worked for themselves. An extract from the *Report of the Children's Employment Commission* of 1843 exposes the young age and long hours worked by some of the children:

> Some little girls begin to work now as early as from six to seven years of age, which is younger than seems to have been the case formerly, and are engaged in general ten hours a-day, exclusive of two hours for meals. Sitting so long on a small stool or bench, with the body in a constrained posture, employed at work which tries the eyes, must be very injurious to Young Children.[17]

Some early drawings of children at work, for example, the depiction of rope making in 1815 [17], are of indifferent draughtsmanship, but illustrate further types of work that were given to children within the broad spread of the textile industry.

[17] Children in a rope factory, 1815.

Paper Making

The manufacture of hand-made paper depended on the supply of rags of linen or cotton as a raw material. Mixed rags required to be sorted after their arrival at the mill and for this task women were usually employed. There are records that children also engaged in this part of paper-making at the end of the eighteenth century, sometimes starting at the age of eight,[18] and sometimes between the ages of ten and twelve.[19]

Brick Making

Brick making was often undertaken by families, including children [18], but with industrialisation and the expanding demand for bricks for building a number of brick-works were established. Children of eight or nine, occasionally younger, were in employment and the working day lasted around thirteen hours. It was estimated that between 20,000 and 30,000 children were working in the brickyards. While brick-making was largely carried out in England, some did take place in Scotland and the Census of 1861 includes a few children under the age of ten working in the occupation category of 'brickmaker.'

Issues of the *Graphic* in 1871 highlighted the plight of children employed in the brick-fields and brick-works, not yet covered by the Factory Acts.[20] The types of toil undertaken by the children were illustrated and included carrying lumps of clay of considerable weight to the brick maker, wheeling heavy loads of bricks in a barrow and tending to the brick kilns [19]. The bare feet, ragged clothes and grim surroundings underscore the artistic intention to draw public attention to the harrowing conditions of these child workers.

[18] Family brick making, 1876.

[19] Children carrying clay in a brickyard.
From *The Graphic*, 1871.

Other Employment in Industrial Urban Areas

The range of employment available for children in the towns and cities of Scotland was extensive. In addition to those considered above, nail-making, match-making, printing and bookbinding, shoe-making and work in chemical works, shipyards, glass works, potteries, and tobacco factories are all referred to in the *Report of the Children's Employment Commission (Trades and Manufactures)* of 1843. This report also provides information on the ages at which children were found in employment and the hours worked. Examples of occupations investigated include:

Nail Manufacture   East of Scotland   Age — 6+

In the manufacture of nails, which is carried out extensively in the East of Scotland, chiefly in the neighbourhood of Camelon and St. Ninian's, Stirlingshire, great numbers of children are employed at a very early age, many when not older than six.[21]

Tobacco Manufacture   age — 7   most start at 8   oldest 12 or 13

In the West of Scotland the Sub-Commissioner reports that Children are employed in this manufacture at a younger age than in any other species of public work except card-setting; that some begin before they are seven years old, but the majority about the age of eight, and that the oldest employed are about twelve or thirteen.[22]

Printing and Bookbinding   10+   7 am — 7.30 pm   or 10 p.m

At Glasgow, in two establishments visited by Mr.Tancred, children are employed at ten years old and upwards from seven A.M. to half-past seven P.M., in cutting, folding and stitching etc. Sometimes, when many periodicals are to be got ready together, these hours extended as late as ten P.M.[23]

[20] Cobbler, c.1865.

Photographs of children working at shoe-making [20] and as part of a shipyard workforce [21] are illustrated. Engravings of children in chemical works [22], glass works [23] and a pottery [24] are also shown.

[21] Management and workers, Alexander Hall & Sons, Aberdeen, 1862.

[22] Work in an alum factory.
From *Chemistry, Theoretical, Practical and Analytical, as Applied and Relating to the Arts and Manufactures* by Sheridan Muspratt, Glasgow, 1860.

[23] Glass making.
From *Chemistry, Theoretical, Practical and Analytical,
as Applied and Relating to the Arts and Manufactures*
by Sheridan Muspratt, Glasgow, 1860.

[24] Work in pottery factory.
From *Chemistry, Theoretical, Practical and Analytical,
as Applied and Relating to the Arts and Manufactures*
by Sheridan Muspratt, Glasgow, 1860.

A further illustration of the range of occupations in which children worked is contained in the report for Greenock in the *New Statistical Account* which comments on the employment of boys in the industries of iron works, sugar refining, sail-cloth manufacture, rope works, potteries, breweries and cooper-work.[24]

Boys also worked extensively in the quarrying industry with, for example, the slate quarries of Caithness providing jobs for considerable numbers.[25]

Chimney Sweeping

The use of children to sweep chimneys by acting as human brushes began in England in the earlier part of the eighteenth century, but was not a practice in Scotland until the end of the century. The climbing boys were usually unwanted children, either paupers apprenticed to their masters by parish authorities or sold by their parents for a few guineas. The starting age was usually from six to eight, but some were apprenticed as young as four or five. In addition to the fear of the dark and the suffocating narrow flues, the boys suffered severely from sores on their elbows and knees. A further and particularly dangerous part of their work was to attempt to extinguish fires in chimneys. Additionally, some of the apprentices had to cry in the street to advertise their masters' trade. The misery of these children was compounded by the infrequent washing and the uncomfortable living conditions. The frequent cruelty of their masters is attested to in many accounts.

Deaths of climbing boys were not uncommon, usually due to suffocation. The *Aberdeen Chronicle* of August 1817 reported the proceedings of the High Court of Justiciary in Edinburgh held on 22nd July of that year which culminated in the conviction of a master-sweep of culpable homicide following the death of one of his apprentice boys stuck in a flue. A rope had been tied to his leg to pull him out, but in spite of the use of such force that the rope broke the boy could not be moved. In the evidence given by a fellow apprentice it was stated that the master-sweep had on occasions stripped the boy, flogged him until he was bleeding and then put salt brine into the wounds. Sometimes he was kept for many hours in a vent. The master-sweep was sentenced to fourteen years' transportation.[26]

Quoted in James Montgomery's *The Chimney-Sweepers Friend and Climbing Boy's Album* under 'Instances of Oppression and Cruelty' was the case of a boy sent up a chimney and because he did not respond to the call of his master another boy was ordered to descend from the top of the flue and meet him halfway. As he was unable to do this, the brick-work in the lower part of the flue was opened and the first boy found dead. The boy in the upper part of the flue called for help, saying he was completely jammed. A bricklayer was sent for, but only obtained a lifeless boy. This double climbing boy death was illustrated in the book [25].

[25] Death of two climbing boys in the flue of a chimney.
From *The Chimney-Sweeper's Friend and Climbing Boy's Album* by James Montgomery, London, 1824.

While the subject of boy sweeps did not attract the interest of painters, the emotive nature of the abuse led to many representations of aspects of their employment in books and periodicals. These covered small boys being sold as apprentices by parents or workhouses [26], being led through the streets by their master and crying in the street to advertise their services. The threat of being forced into apprenticeship to a chimney-sweep was portrayed in the Charles Dickens novel *Oliver Twist* by the artist George Cruickshank in an illustration that featured both humour and pathos [27].

[26] Widow selling her son to a chimney-sweep.
From *The Chimney-Sweeper's Friend and Climbing Boy's Album* by James Montgomery, London, 1824.

[27] "Oliver escapes being bound apprentice to the sweep".
Illustration by George Cruickshank for *Oliver Twist* by Charles Dickens, London, 1862.

Street Trading and Casual Employment

In addition to trades and manufacturing, mining and quarrying, the use of children was widespread for running errands or for street trading, selling such articles as flowers, matches, newspapers and firewood [28]. Street trading by children has been represented by both illustrators and painters. *The Lucifer Match Girl* [29], an illustration from Mayhew's *London Labour and the London Poor*, depicts a small girl, adequately clothed, but glum and resigned in demeanour. *The Paper Seller* by Charles Sellar [30] is a half-length portrait of a boy with papers under his arm: there is no implication in the painting of deprivation or poverty. John Burr painted a scene showing a woman outside her door being offered goods by a very small boy and an older girl. In this picture, *The Little Boy Vendor*,[27] there is no indication of hardship; both children being depicted as well clad and shod.

Some children hung about railway stations hoping to earn a few pennies carrying bags, some worked as shoe shine boys and others collected scrap from rubbish heaps to sell. In Dundee up to the 1860s poor children were employed as street cleaners to remove mud, horse dung and refuse from the streets, and in areas of the city where coal was dumped outside the houses children were paid to shift it into basement stores.[28]

[28] Edinburgh street hawkers. From *Child Slaves of Britain* by Robert Sherard, London, 1905.

[29] Lucifer match girl.
From *London Labour and the London Poor* by Henry Mayhew, London, 1851.

[30] Charles Sellar, *The Paper Seller*.

Part-time Employment out of School Hours

With the implementation of the *Education (Scotland)* Act of 1872, making attendance at school from the ages of five to thirteen compulsory, the first experience of work for many children in the towns of the late nineteenth century was a part-time job out of school hours. Some took on a paper round or a milk round in the mornings. Others acted as message boys or helped as van-boys. Bundling sticks for use in kindling fires could also bring in a few pence [31].

Robert Sherard in his *The Child Slaves of Britain* published in 1905 quotes the Glasgow School Board finding that over 4000 children attending Glasgow schools were employed out of school hours. Most had employment carrying milk or bread in the mornings and working for shops in the evenings. Some hired out their services to clean stairs, others worked at home on such tasks as shirt-finishing or paper-bag making. It was claimed that a number of children were working up to fifty hours a week out of school hours. The abuse of medical certification to gain exemption from school attendance, so that work at home or elsewhere could be pursued, was said to occur.

[31] Two girls binding wood.

41

[32] Boy caddies.
From the Washington Wilson Collection.

At golf courses close to towns boys could obtain employment as caddies [32]. The popularity of the sport made it an attractive subject for artists and an example is seen in William Darling McKay's *Golfing on Bruntsfield Links* where each golfer is accompanied by one or more boy caddies [33].

[33] William Darling McKay, *Golfing on Bruntsfield Links*.

Chapter 3

Employment in Agricultural and Rural Areas

Child labour in the countryside in the nineteenth century contrasted with that in the industrial towns and cities in a number of ways. Many of the children worked in a family setting or for farmers in the area of their homes rather than being under the control of impersonal factory owners and overseers. Apprenticed children from workhouses were not used for rural occupations.

The conditions under which the children worked in the country were environmentally much healthier with better food and freedom from the dust, heat and noise of the textile factories or the dark and damp of the mines. The stunted growth, bony deformities and lung disease seen in many of the factory children were seldom present in those working in the country. While the work undertaken by children in the country could be hard or monotonous it was usually seasonal and allowed at least partial school education.

Farming Activities

In the agricultural districts of Scotland the presence of children alongside parents or older siblings working on the land was commonplace [34].

[34] Young farmworkers, Perthshire, 1904.

[35] Robert McGregor, *Tending the Family Cow*.

Paintings such as Alexander Mann's *The Gleaner*[28] and Robert McGregor's *Tending the Family Cow* [35] show children of tender years in fields where work was being undertaken.

Information on the employment of children in agriculture in different districts of Scotland is included in the *Report of the Commission on the Employment of Children, Young Persons, and Women in Agriculture* of 1870.[29] Typical statements were:

> The employment in agriculture of boys and girls, many under 10 years of age, is very general in this county. For thinning turnips, weeding, and bird tenting, the labour of children from 9 to 10 years of age is almost as useful as that of those of more advanced age. They are too young to use the hoe, but after a little practice they thin turnips with the hand very quickly and dexterously.[30]

> The work for children consists of setting potatoes, herding stock as soon as the grass begins to grow, thinning turnips with a hoe, then harvest and potato gathering. Very few are employed in scaring birds in the spring. I think about half the children of from 9 or 10 upwards are employed in these occupations.[31]

Boys and girls are employed on most of the arable farms, from 11 or 12 to 15 years of age, in weeding potatoes and in singling and cleaning turnips, the strongest boys are also employed in hay-making, and in harvest they lift the grain after the machine and put it into sheaf and at the season for taking up potatoes they are also extensively employed.[32]

Child employment followed the seasonal cycle of farming activities with its need for extra hands, particularly for spring, summer and autumn work. Work in the turnip fields required the help of children as shown in William Darling McKay's *The Turnip Field*.[33] Among the other common occupations that engaged children were herding, bird scaring, haymaking, potato picking and, at harvest time, gleaning. All these were represented by artists in modes ranging from the realistic to the sentimental.

Herding

Herding livestock was one aspect of farm work for which children were always required. This entailed tending the animals to confine them to their own particular pasture and prevent them from straying on to crops. This theme was explored by numerous artists.

David Fulton painted a pair of pictures, *The Young Shepherdess* and *The Cow Herd*,[34] depicting a girl and a boy with sheep or cattle respectively in the background. In each painting the child gazes directly at the viewer and the general impression is of the sentimental treatment of an occupation that must have been frequently uncomfortable and monotonous. The engraving of a sketch of herd boys on Iona from an issue of the *Illustrated London News* dated 1847 captures these features [36].

[36] Herd boys on Iona. Sketch by M. Gavarni in *The Illustrated London News*, 1849.

[37] Edward Walton, *The Young Shepherd*.

A further representation of a child engaged in herding was provided by Edward A. Walton: in his watercolour entitled *The Young Shepherd* a boy sits, stick in hand, with his charges behind [37]. Quite different in presentation, but typical of the artist, is Edward Hornel's *The Cowherd* in which the girl herd and her little companion sit close to the picture plane while the background is flattened.[35] This is a colourful picture, loosely painted and with no pretence of realism. James Guthrie's *To Pastures New* (Aberdeen Art Gallery) depicts the care of a flock of geese by a girl.

Bird Scaring

Bird scaring to prevent crows, pigeons or other birds interfering with and damaging crops was an occupation frequently given to children. It is featured in a number of magazine illustrations, principally from England, that show children with either a rattle, as in *The Little Scarecrow* [38], or a gun as in the example from the *Illustrated London News*.[36]

[38] T. Dicksee, *The Little Scarecrow*. From *The Graphic*, 1857.

Haymaking

Turning the swathes of mown grass to help the drying process and then forking them into a stack were tasks undertaken by both children and adults [39].

[39] Family farming group, Selkirk, c.1900.

Assistance in gathering in the hay is implied by John Burr's *A Haymaker* [40]; a girl painted with a wistful expression stands in a field with a hay fork over one shoulder carrying a small pitcher.

[40] John Burr, *A Haymaker*.

Potato Picking

The autumn task of lifting potatoes has provided employment to children for centuries: a typical scene is shown in the archival photograph [41]. Robert McGregor's *The Last of the Potatoes* features a girl emptying a basket of potatoes into a bag held by a younger boy, while a small girl holds out her pinafore, presumably containing more gathered potatoes. An old man with a basket and fork looks on while a woman carrying a basket makes her way towards a cottage in the background [42].

[41] Lifting potatoes, Fifeshire, c.1900.

[42] Robert McGregor, *The Last of the Potatoes.*

Gleaning

Gleaning, the gathering of ears of corn left by the reapers, was a task often left to women and children. *Gleaners*, painted by Hugh Cameron, shows four children in a field: two carry sheaves of wheat and the other two are bending to pick from the ground [43]. Also entitled *Gleaners* (Dundee Art Gallery), the same artist has painted a woman with a large bundle of wheat on her back while holding the hand of a small child; two other children carry bundles of wheat and an older child carries a baby on her back. *An Arrochar Gleaner* [44] is a

[43] Hugh Cameron, *Gleaners*.

[44] Robert Herdman, *An Arrochar Gleaner*.

typical example of Robert Herdman's romanticised representation of the poor in rural life, showing a young and pretty girl resting with a sheaf of wheat on her back. Charles Hardie's *Gleaners* (Queensland Art Gallery, Brisbane) has a number of figures in a harvested field with a village in the background. A woman in the foreground of the picture holds a sheaf of corn, a girl plays with a baby on the ground, and other children gather harvest remains over the field. William Darling McKay's *Where the Gleaners Rest* depicts three children, two of them bare-footed, sitting on a bank close to the picture plane; in the background small groups of adults stand in the harvested field.[37] It is a picture characteristic of McKay's rendering of rural realism with a freedom from sentimentality.

Pastoral Activities

Children participated in a variety of pastoral activities peripheral to agriculture. In some instances a meagre wage was obtained; in others the work undertaken by children was an important contribution in the family's struggle against poverty. Jobs in a pastoral setting included the cutting and drying of peat, bark stripping, collecting manure, gathering brushwood and ferns, and picking berries and other fruit. Sometimes boys helped the local blacksmith [45].

[45] Smithy, Shetlands, c.1905.

Peat Cutting

A main source of fuel for many families was peat. The semi-carbonised decayed vegetable matter found under the surface of boggy moorland was cut into brick-shaped pieces and set out to dry. Children assisted by laying out the peats and turning them to facilitate the drying process. It was frequently a family activity [46]. William Stewart MacGeorge's *A Galloway Peat Moss* depicts a group including young girls working at the peats [47].

[46] Family at the peats, Loch Fannich, Ross-shire, 1890.

Comments from the *Commission on the Employment of Children in Agriculture* of 1870 included:

> One of the principal employments for which children are employed is laying out the peats when the parents cut them. This employment a child be fit for at 8; it is the earliest work in the year for which they are taken from school; after that comes weeding and hoeing; then September holidays and harvest, then potato-lifting, which is the great wind-up, and that brings the work into the middle of November.[38]

> The children begin to leave school to go out to work at 10, for the summer months: besides going out to the regular work a great many go out in the mossing time (i.e. when the peat is cut for firing); that is, not so much to work for hire as for their parents; the children are employed in turning the peats over and spreading them. The farm servants generally have the privilege of cutting peats.[39]

[47] William Stewart MacGeorge, *A Galloway Peat Moss*.

Bark Stripping

The use of vegetable tannins for converting animal hide or skin into leather has been known from ancient times, and the Hebrews used oak bark, a relatively rich source of tannins, for the process. Bark stripping was one of the occupations that gave employment to children and was mentioned in the returns from a number of areas in the *Commission's Report* of 1870:

> In the wooded districts of Dumfries-shire there is a good deal of barking, which gives employment for a month or two in the spring to children of from 9 to 12 years of age. They go into the woods, taking with them their food for the day, in parties of 20 or 30 in company with women under the charge of a male superintendent who contracts to do a certain quantity of work.[40]

> The summer work takes the boys away more than the girls. There is a good deal of wood here and some of the boys go away for barking about this time (May); that does not detain them long, and the ordinary work is herding.[41]

Artistic depiction of the activity is rare, but Hector Chalmers' *The Bark Strippers* [48] shows a boy in the foreground carrying a load of bark on his back. Stripped trees lie on the ground and a number of adult workers are in the background.

[48] Hector Chalmers, *The Bark Strippers*.

Manure Collecting

The collection of manure, used as a fertiliser for garden or field, was sometimes carried out by children. Although the painting by William Darling McKay has been entitled *Children Playing Outside a Village* at some date in its history [49], it is suggested that the scene is more accurately interpreted as showing two boys gathering cow pats, one with a spade and the other standing by a barrow.

[49] William Darling McKay, *Children Playing Outside a Village*.

Wood Gathering

Wood was a common source of fuel, but gathering brushwood for fuel implies marked poverty [50]. The artistic representations of this labour by both Hugh Cameron and Robert McGregor are in accord with this implication. In Robert McGregor's *Gathering Winter Fuel* [51] a weary-looking woman carries a small child along a woodland path followed by a boy dragging a bundle of wood. Robert McGregor's painting *Gathering Driftwood* shows a woman holding a baby in her arms in a landscape of sand dunes while a young child at her side carries a bundle of driftwood [52]. Hugh Cameron's painting *Wha Drudge and Drive Through Wet and Dry the Hale Day Lang* is similar in sentiment,[42] providing an image of a tired young mother walking along a moorland path. She has a sack on her back and is accompanied by two bare-footed children, one with a basket and the other carrying a bundle of brushwood.

[50] Bringing home firewood, Morar, c.1905.

[51] Robert McGregor, *Gathering Winter Fuel*.

[52] Robert McGregor, *Gathering Driftwood*.

Fern Gathering

Gathering ferns or bracken to be used for animal bedding was a task frequently assigned to children [53]. Robert Herdman's *Young Girl* [54] depicts this pastoral activity, showing a girl sitting on a rock in a country landscape with a bundle of ferns on her back.

[53] Bringing home bracken.

[54 Robert Herdman, *Young Girl*.

[55] William McTaggart and John McWhirter, *The Bramble Gatherers*.

Berry Picking

The gathering of berries was often for personal or family consumption, although paid berry picking has become a popular temporary job for young people. Scenes of child berry pickers made attractive subjects for paintings and there are abundant examples. Illustrated is the painting executed jointly by William McTaggart and John McWhirter [55]. Others include David Fulton's *Bramble Time*,[43] Robert McGregor's *Blackberry Pickers*,[44] and William McTaggart's group of four children entitled *The Blackberry Pickers*.[45]

[56] Fisher boys, Newhaven, c.1856.

[57] Women and children baiting lines, St Andrews, c.1850.

Chapter 4
Employment in Coastal and Fishing Areas

Child employment in the coastal areas was embedded in the culture of the close-knit fishing communities. Although life was harsh and frequently dangerous, boys went to sea with their fathers as soon as they were able to provide help. A number of the historic calotypes of Hill and Adamson featured images of fisher boys [56].

Traditionally the whole family was involved in the labours related to fishing. Baiting the fishing lines was usually undertaken by women, often assisted by their children [57] or performed by children alone [58]. Girls learned various other skills from their mothers which enabled them to share the workload while also preparing them for their future role as wives of fishermen. The range of work available to the young included the collection of shellfish, the preparation of shellfish for use as bait [1], digging for other forms of bait such as lugworms [59] and seaweed-gathering. Girls could also be required to help with the mending of nets. In all these ways children could supplement the family income.

[58] Baiting the lines, Auchmithie, c.1895.

[59] Digging for bait, Saltcoats, Ayrshire.

Boys could be given work at sea and the early age of starting work on fishing boats is noted in the memoirs of David Hawthorn Cardno: he began as a scum boy on a small sail boat fishing for herring off Peterhead in the 1860s collecting any fish that escaped from the nets as they were hauled in.[46] The photograph of the crew of a fishing boat leaving from Peterhead around 1860 includes a number of boys [60]. Some boys served on ocean-going ships including the whalers. Cardno recounts his attempts to stow away on a whaler beginning at the age of about eleven years: apparently this was a relatively common practice among boys.[47]

The combination of children and attractive localities was a popular subject for Scottish artists of the nineteenth and early twentieth centuries. This resulted in numerous paintings of children involved in such tasks as mussel collecting, kelp gathering, fishing and unloading the catch from boats.

Shellfish Gathering

The collection of shellfish was a frequent occupation for children in the fishing areas. While some was used for food, much was collected as bait for fishing lines.

[60] Crew of fishing vessel, Peterhead, c.1860.

The Report of the Royal Commission on Employment of Children of 1870 included:

> Besides peat-cutting and agricultural labour there are various
> local employments that take away the children of particular
> districts in Argyllshire; of these whelk-gathering is most
> prominent; it employs the very smallest children about the
> coasts of Mull and the adjacent mainland in the month of
> March. "Children will go at 8 and 9 and 10 to the whelks;
> can be seen in droves going away with their mothers and
> older people. Look like gipsies or the like of them, not well
> dressed; get wet on the shore; they say sea-water is good for
> them". They make sometimes 2s. a day at this work. In like
> manner little children go out to gather tangle in the Island
> of Tyree after the great storms, and are out at 9 or 10 years
> of age in shocking weather.[48]

The collection by children of edible shellfish and material suitable for baiting
fish-lines has been featured by several painters. Children with baskets, sometimes
alone and sometimes with adults, at the seashore or among rock pools were
popular subjects for William Marshall Brown. Examples of these paintings of
life in the east coast fishing communities are *When the Tide is Out*,[49] *Young
Mussel Gatherers*,[50] *The Mussel Gatherers* [62] and *Catching Crabs*.[51] Robert
McGregor in his *Gathering Mussels* has a group of adults and children engaged
in the same task painted with his characteristic unsentimental realism.[52]

[62] William Marshall Brown, *The Mussel Gatherers*.

With William McTaggart's favoured motifs of children and seascapes, shellfish and bait gathering have, predictably, been subjects for his paintings. In *The Bait Gatherers* [62] a small boy carrying a basket and stick scans the water around rock pools at the edge of the sea watched by two companions. This painting belongs to William McTaggart's earlier style with clear demarcation of the figures although the handling is looser than that of most of his contemporaries who painted genre subjects. In contrast, in *Shrimpers* ,[53] dated later at 1893, the figures at the sea edge are partly dissolved and no details can be discerned.

[62] William McTaggart, *The Bait Gatherers*.

Kelp Gathering

Kelp, a form of seaweed widely used as a fertilizer in the Highlands of Scotland, was gathered on the beaches and rocks, particularly after storms at sea washed quantities of it ashore. Its collection provided one source of work for children recorded in photograph [63] and depicted on canvas by Robert McGregor in his *Kelp Gatherers*.[54] In this painting carts are being drawn along the sands by donkeys or oxen accompanied by girls or young women. William Marshall Brown's *Gathering Kelp* [64] shows two children standing on the rocks by the sea; the girl is emptying seaweed from a bucket into a bag held by the boy.

[63] Collecting seaweed, East coast of Scotland, c.1900.

[64] William Marshall Brown, *Gathering Kelp*.

Fishing

The young assisted with sea fishing in a number of ways. They helped to unload the catch from the fishing boats, a theme which has been a subject for a number of Scottish artists. The presence of children at such work is a component of William McTaggart's *The Fishers Landing* [65]; a woman carries a basket in one hand and a baby on her other arm while a girl stoops over a large basket closer to the shore. In the background are small fishing boats and fishermen at the water's edge.

[65] William McTaggart, *The Fishers Landing*.

In addition to baiting lines, children also on occasions fished with rod and line themselves, although this was often a leisure activity: a fine example is William McTaggart's *Fisher Children* [66]. William Marshall Brown's *The Fishing Lesson* shows a group of figures fishing from rocks at the edge of the sea: a boy wields a rod on his own while an old fisherman helps a small boy to hold his rod.[55] In John Burr's *The Young Fishers* a boy stoops at the water's edge, rod in one hand and a net in the other, while a girl sits on the edge of a beached boat with a number of fish on the sand by her feet.[56] Three small boys in a boat some distance off the shore dangle their lines over the stern in William McTaggart's *The Little Anglers* [67]. Preparing a line while he sits in a boat is a fisher boy's occupation in Robert Noble's *Reddin' the Line* [68].

[66] William McTaggart, *Fisher Children*.

[67] William McTaggart, *The Young Fishers*.

[68] Robert Noble, *Reddin' the Line*.

[69] William McTaggart, *The Old Net*.

Net Making and Mending

Nets were fundamental in securing a good catch of fish. Some fisher families made their own nets and children contributed to the process of weaving the rows of meshes. Where nets were produced commercially girls were employed in the net factories. Maintaining the nets in good condition was also important and children assisted in laying the nets out to dry and repairing those that were damaged. William McTaggart in *The Old Net* has portrayed an elderly fisherman sewing a net while a boy and a girl sit close by helping by holding up the net [69].

Going to Sea

The departure of a boy to join a ship at sea to work is the theme of William McTaggart's *Going to Sea* [70]. He is painted bare-footed with his few belongings tied into a small bundle looking wistfully back at his home while the family dog sniffs his hand. An older mariner looks over the pier while in the background is a three-masted ship and a boat being rowed towards the shore.

[70] William McTaggart, *Going to Sea*.

Chapter 5

Employment in the Home

Many girls were required to provide help in the home. Some, even at an early age, were sent as domestic servants to another home for a small wage and their keep, but the majority only supplemented the family income by giving their mother the opportunity to provide labour on the family croft or to take paid employment elsewhere.

The wide range of jobs imposed on young girls in an agricultural domestic setting is underscored by the description of Janet Bathgate, a shepherd's daughter, hired at the age of seven in the early years of the nineteenth century. These *age 7* included herding the cow, fetching and carrying peats, taking warm milk to the lambs, cleaning out the byre, digging up potatoes and washing them in the burn, sweeping out the house and washing the dishes.[57]

Care of Younger Children

Baby-minding was a task traditionally given to girls [71]. Looking after younger brothers or sisters was a particularly common responsibility and was the subject of a number of paintings by nineteenth century Scottish artists. One example, *Sisters*, painted by Hugh Cameron, shows a sombre little girl carrying her baby sister along a paved path with a basket on her arm.[58] A number of

[71] Babyminding, Renfrewshire, c.1890.

[72] Robert McGregor, *Breakfast Time.*

paintings incorporate an additional incident related to the care of the younger child such as feeding as in Robert McGregor's *Breakfast Time* [72]. The action of this painting is set in a cottage and shows a little girl feeding a yet younger child while another girl proffers a spoonful from a pan.

A repeated theme is of a mother returning to find the young carer asleep. In John Burr's *Asleep on Duty* a woman looks round the open door of a cottage at a child asleep on a chair with an infant in a cot nearby.[59] A further example of this theme by the same artist is *The Careless Nurse* (Dundee Art Gallery).

Domestic Work

Domestic tasks undertaken by children and represented by artists include washing clothes and dishes, the preparation of food, polishing, sewing and winding wool. William Dyce included in his painting *A Scene in Arran* children helping their mother with washing in a stream, rescuing buckets being washed away [73]. Hugh Cameron's *The Little Housewife* features a small girl standing on a stool to wash a dish in a basin [74]. In Robert Gemmell Hutchison's *The Young Housewife* a girl is peeling potatoes in a bowl,[60] while the same artist in *Winding Wool* shows a little girl holding a hank of pink wool while her companion winds it off into a ball.[61] In a further painting by Gemmell Hutchison a small child polishes a kettle.[62]

[73] William Dyce, *A Scene in Arran*.

[74] Hugh Cameron, *The Little Housewife*.

An extension of domestic duties from within the home included the running of errands, feeding the poultry and fetching water from the well. In Hugh Cameron's *Responsibility* a child is being handed a shopping basket by her mother [75]. A picture by William Darling McKay, *Feeding the Poultry* [76], shows three well-dressed children feeding a few turkeys and hens. Children feeding poultry

[75] Hugh Cameron, *Responsibility*.

[76] William Darling McKay, *Feeding the Poultry*.

is the theme of John Lochhead's *In the Farmyard* [77], while scattering grain from a basket to a small flock of hens and a duck is also the subject of Robert Gemmell Hutchison's *Feeding the Chickens*.[63] Help in gathering vegetables is featured in James Guthrie's renowned *The Hind's Daughter* [78]. Children at a well are prominent in paintings such as William McTaggart's The Old Pump Well (Stirling Smith Art Gallery and Museum), Hugh Cameron's *The Village Well* (Aberdeen Art Gallery) and Hannah McGoun's *Children at the Well* [79].

[77] John Lockhead, *In the Farmyard*.

[78] James Guthrie, *The Hind's Daughter*.

[79] Hannah Preston McGoun, *Children at the Well*.

The practice of children taking food to workers in the field or wood was widespread and is recorded in photograph [80]. It also provided subject matter for paintings by a number of artists. In Thomas Faed's *The Woodcutter's Children* [81] a weary-looking man with axe in hand sits on a tree-trunk while the older of two girls pours a drink for him from a pitcher into a mug.

[80] Boy carrying pitchers to field workers, c.1905.

[81] Thomas Faed, *The Woodcutter's Children*.

Notes

1. *Education Commission (Scotland). Report on the State of Education in Glasgow,* p.21.

2. *Seventh Decennial Census of the Population on Scotland. III. Occupations of the People of Scotland,* 1861.

3. *Eighth Decennial Census of the Population of Scotland. XIV. Occupations of the Inhabitants of Scotland,* 1871.

4. *Report of the Children's Employment Commission (Mines), Parliamentary Papers,* 1842.

5. Ibid, p.197.

6. Ibid, p.198.

7. Ibid, p.200.

8. Ibid, p.238.

9. *Report from the Select Committee on the "Bill" to Regulate the Labour of Children in the Mills and Factories of the United Kingdom. The Minutes of Evidence, Parliamentary Papers,* 1832.

10. *From Chapters in the Life of a Dundee Factory Boy. Quoted in The Dundee Book. An Anthology of Living in the City,* ed. Billy Kay, Edinburgh, 1995, p.81.

11. *The Statistical Account of Scotland (OSA),* Edinburgh, 1791-1799, VII, pp.850 1 (Abbey Parish of Paisley, Renfrewshire).

12. *New Statistical Account of Scotland (NSA),* Edinburgh, 1845, XI, p.26 (Dundee, Forfarshire).

13. NSA, VI, p.697 (Govan, Lanarkshire).

14. *Report of the Children's Employment Commission (Trades and Manufactures), Parliamentary Papers,* 1843, p.14.

15. Ibid, p.13.

16. *NSA,* VIII, p.226 (Bonhill, Dumbartonshire).

17. *Report of Children's Employment Commission,* 1843, p.124.

18. *OSA,* III, p.11 (Ayton, Berwickshire).

19. Ibid, II, p.203 (Currie, Midlothian).

20. *Graphic,* Vol.3, 1871, pp.491 and 534.

21. *Children's Employment Commission,* 1843, p.8.

22. Ibid, p.15.

23. Ibid, p.135.

23. *NSA,* VII, p.439 (Greenock, Renfrewshire).

24. *Education Commission (Scotland). Report on the State of Education in the Country Districts,*1866, p.220-1.

25. Quoted in K.H.Strange, *Climbing Boys,* 1982.

26. John Burr, *The Little Boy Vendor*, Christie's, Edinburgh, 18 Nov. 1993, Lot 890.

27. R. Lamont-Brown and P. Adamson, *Victorian and Edwardian Dundee and Broughty Ferry from Rare Photographs*, St Andrews, 1981, p.68.

28. Alexander Mann, *The Gleaners*, Christie's, Edinburgh, 31 Oct. 2002, Lot 104.

29. *Royal Commission on the Employment of Children, Young Persons, and Women in Agriculture. Fourth Report,* 1870.

30. Ibid, *Appendix Part I*, p.91.

31. Ibid, *Appendix Part II*, p.19.

32. Ibid, *Appendix Part I*, p.96.

33. William Darling McKay, *The Turnip Field*, Sotheby's, Belgravia, 2 Oct. 1973, Lot 171.

34. David Fulton, *The Young Shepherdess* and *The Cow Herd*, Christie's, Glasgow, 2 Feb. 1994, Lots 469 and 478.

35. Edward Hornel, *The Cowherd*, Phillips, Edinburgh, 8 Dec. 2001, Lot 15.

36. Crow Scaring. Illustration by Phiz entitled 'The Crow-Boy' in *The Illustrated London News*, Vol.20, 21 Dec. 1850.

37. William Darling McKay, *Where Gleaners Rest*, Sotheby's, London, 28 Aug. 1975, Lot 321.

38. *Royal Commission on the Employment of Children, Young Persons, and Women in Agriculture. Fourth Report. Appendix Part I*, 1870, p.113.

39. Ibid, *Appendix Part II*, p.35.

40. Ibid, *Appendix Part I*, p.84.

41. Ibid, *Appendix Part II*, p.41.

42. Hugh Cameron, *Wha Drudge and Drive Through Wet and Dry the Hale Day Lang*, Sotheby's, Gleneagles, 1 Sept. 1999, Lot 1189.

43. David Fulton, *Bramble Time*, Sotheby's, London, 21 May, 1986, Lot 17.

44. Robert McGregor, *Blackberry Pickers*, Sotheby's, Belgravia, 26 March 1974, Lot 214.

45. William McTaggart, The Blackberry Pickers, Christie's, London, 29 July 1977, Lot 72.

46. Gavin Sutherland (ed.), *A Whaler's Tale. The Memoirs of David Hawthorn Cardno of Peterhead 1853-1938*, Aberdeenshire Council, 1996, p.1.

47. Ibid, pp.1-2.

48. *Royal Commission on Employment of Children, Young Persons and Women in Agriculture, Appendix Part I*, 1870, p.115.

49. William Marshall Brown, *When the Tide is Out*, Christie's, Glasgow, 19 Nov. 1992, Lot 72.

50. William Marshall Brown, *Young Mussel Gatherers*, Sotheby's, London, 24 Aug. 1976, Lot 424.

51. William Marshall Brown, *Catching Crab*, Christie's, Glasgow, 22 Nov. 1989, Lot 593.

52. Robert McGregor, *Gathering Mussels*, Sotheby's, Hopetoun House, 27 March 1984, Lot 382.

53. William McTaggart, *Shrimpers*, Sotheby's, Hopetoun House, 27 March 1984, Lot 562.

54. Robert McGregor, *Kelp Gatherers*, Sotheby's, Hopetoun House, 27 March 1984, Lot 379.

55. William Marshall Brown, *The Fishing Lesson*, Christie's, Scotland, 11 Dec. 1986, Lot 31.

56. John Burr, *The Young Fishers*, Christie's, Edinburgh, 18 Nov. 1993, Lot 890.

57. J. Bathgate, *Aunt Janet's Legacy to her Nieces*, 5th edit., Selkirk, 1901, p.53.

58. Hugh Cameron, *Sisters*, Christie's, Glasgow, 30 Oct. 1997, Lot 856.

59. John Burr, *Asleep on Duty*, Christie's, London, 6 June 1980, Lot 51.

60. Robert Gemmell Hutchison, *The Young Housewife*, Sotheby's, Hopetoun House, 25 April 1989, Lot 202.

61. Robert Gemmell Hutchison, *Winding Wool*, Sotheby's, Glasgow, 9 Dec. 1997, Lot 105.

62. Robert Gemmell Hutchison, *Polishing the Kettle*, Sotheby's, Gleneagles, 27 August 2003, Lot 1196.

63. Robert Gemmell Hutchison, *Feeding the Chickens*, Sotheby's, Hopetoun House, 27 March 1984. Lot 505.

Summary and Conclusions

Industrialisation beginning in Britain around 1780 brought additional hardships to generations of poor children. Child labour was not new and had been part of economic life for many centuries, but the need for additional cheap labour in the burgeoning textile mills and the demand for power fuelled by coal led to the exploitation and often brutal treatment of large numbers of children.

The conscience of the nation led to piecemeal legislation throughout the nineteenth century, albeit frequently resisted and delayed by mine and mill owners, to regulate the age at which children could be employed and the number of hours worked in a range of industries: the major Parliamentary Acts concerned are summarised in Chapter 1. It was, however, the passage of the Education Acts in the early 1870s with the obligation on parents to send their children to school that heralded the effective demise of widespread child labour in Britain. Child employment did not end, but was largely confined to part-time work out of school hours.

The visual representation of child employment in the nineteenth century used a number of modes. Paintings, graphic representations in the form of engravings, etchings, woodcuts, and, from the middle of the century, photographs were all produced.

Images of child labour were used for varying purposes. Some graphical material was published throughout the century with the object of influencing public opinion; in other cases it was as a factual record of current affairs. Archival photographs appeared relatively late in the century, too late to capture on film the worst of the abuses of children in the mines and factories, even if access to these had been allowed. Photographs taken in the period when the technique was more widely available have shown children in working environments, for example, as part of a works group, or in a posed portrait. Painters were active throughout the century, but in spite of the popularity of genre scenes they eschewed child exploitation in mine or mill as subject matter. It is probable that this was largely the result of lack of public demand for paintings of such scenes, but it may have been compounded by a reticence of factory owners to permit access by artists to sketch or paint in their premises. Many artists painted children working, but these were almost all in congenial occupations and usually in rural settings, for example, herding, gathering shellfish by the shore, feeding hens or performing domestic duties. In many of the child paintings purporting to illustrate a young person undertaking a specific type of work the occupation is identified only by some associated implement, for example, a hay-fork or a creel. The child is not shown actually working and the linkage with an occupation is principally to provide a background for the portrait of an attractive child. A few Scottish artists, however, did paint realistic scenes of rural work, often including children: particularly notable were Robert McGregor, Hugh Cameron and William Darling McKay.

It is concluded that neither paintings nor photographic archive have contributed greatly to our appreciation of the hardship of child labour in the earlier decades of the nineteenth century in Scotland. In contrast, many of the illustrations produced for book or magazine at the time emphasised the reality of their conditions and treatment, and contributed to the implementation of reforms.

It has become evident in this survey that a direct comparison between the work of artists and the available photographic archive in illustrating child employment in the nineteenth century is subject to a number of caveats. The availability of photography to record everyday life was relatively late in the century whereas the work of artists yielded paintings and drawings of some aspects of these subjects from the beginning of the period. In addition, artists, illustrators and photographers had generally different aims in the production of their images. Nevertheless, the combination of the different modes of presentation provides a further dimension to our understanding of the life of children in nineteenth-century Scotland.

Notes on Artists

William Marshall Brown (1863-1936)

Born in Edinburgh, Marshall Brown worked as a wood engraver and book illustrator while attending evening classes at the Edinburgh School of Art and the Royal Scottish Academy Life School. He later studied at South Kensington. He lived in Edinburgh, but also had a studio at Cocksburnspath, and painted in France and Holland in addition to Scotland. In 1905 he became chairman of the Scottish Society of Artists.

William Marshall Brown painted in both oil and watercolour. Paintings of children playing or working by the shore were one of his favoured motifs; two are illustrated in Figures 63 and 64.

John Burr (1831-93)

A native of Edinburgh, John Burr began painting professionally at the early age of fourteen, moving from town to town in Scotland painting portraits. In his spare time he painted landscapes. Self-taught to the age of nineteen he enrolled at the Trustees' Academy, becoming one of the pupils of Robert Scott Lauder. In 1861 he left Edinburgh to seek greater opportunities in London and resided there for the remainder of his life. He visited Holland in 1869 to study the paintings of the Old Dutch masters. Burr served for several years as President of the Royal Society of British Artists, and exhibited both at the Royal Academy and the Royal Scottish Academy.

John Burr's motifs were principally domestic genre, painted in oil or watercolour. A number had humorous overtones; an example is shown in Figure 75. The popularity of his work is demonstrated by the number of his pictures that were engraved for wide circulation.

Hugh Cameron (1835-1918)

Hugh Cameron, born in Edinburgh, was apprenticed to an architect at the age of fourteen. His interest in art led him to enrol at the Trustees' Academy, becoming one of the pupils of Scott Lauder. In 1870 he met the Hague School artist Josef Israels in Aberdeen and the influence of the Dutch painter can be discerned in his work. Cameron moved to London in 1876 and lived there for the next twelve years. He did, however, spend time in Largo during the summers and in Edinburgh in the winter. He made few trips abroad, but did visit the south of France and Italy.

Hugh Cameron's principal painting motifs were rural genre including, in particular, old women and children; examples are illustrated in Figures 44, 76 and 77. In addition to rural and domestic scenes, he engaged in portraiture.

Hector Chalmers (1848-1943)

Hector Chalmers was an Edinburgh artist who studied at the Trustees' Academy and later at the Royal Scottish Academy School. He painted both in oil and watercolour and his work ranged through figure subjects, genre and portraiture, but landscape was his principal motif.

William Dyce (1806-64)

William Dyce was born in Aberdeen into a medical family. He proceeded to graduate from Marischal College planning to study theology, but his interest turned to art and he joined the Royal Academy Schools in London for a short time. He travelled to Rome at the age of nineteen and stayed almost a year, the first of three visits to Italy. On one of these he had contact with the group of German painters known as the Nazarenes who believed that all art should serve a moral or religious purpose and were involved with the revival of fresco painting. In his later years Dyce was supportive of the work of the Pre-Raphaelite movement.

In the early part of his career portrait painting in Edinburgh provided a livelihood for Dyce. He became an expert in fresco painting and received commissions to decorate rooms in the Houses of Parliament. A vacation in Arran with his family provided subject matter and background scenery for a number of paintings including *Scene in Arran* painted around 1859 and reproduced in Figure 73.

William Dyce undertook a number of administrative duties in art education including the joint Mastership of the Trustees' Academy and the post of Superintendent of the Government Schools of Design in London. A man of wide interests Dyce was involved in early church music and the design of stained glass windows.

Thomas Faed (1826-1900)

Thomas Faed was one of the artistic children of a millwright living at Gatehouse-of-Fleet in Kirkcudbrightshire. After a short spell as an apprentice draper in Castle Douglas he went at the age of seventeen to join his brother John, a miniature painter in Edinburgh. He became a student at the Trustees' Academy where he studied under Sir William Allan and Thomas Duncan. His ability was attested by the award of a prize in the life class of 1847. He began to exhibit pictures at the Royal Scottish Academy in 1844 and at the Royal Academy in 1851. In the following year he left Edinburgh to make his home in London.

Thomas Faed painted in both oil and watercolour. Rural life and domestic genre constituted his principal subjects; an example is shown in Figure 81. He also painted portraits. A number of his genre paintings received wide public acclaim.

Sir James Guthrie (1859-1939)

James Guthrie was born at Greenock, the son of the Rev. John Guthrie, one of the founders of the Evangelical Union Church. He began law studies at the University of Glasgow, but turned to art when he was aged eighteen. In the summer of 1879 he painted at Rosneath on the Clyde coast with Edward Walton and Joseph Crawhall, the first of a number of summers spent painting with others of the group of artists who became known as the Glasgow Boys. Later in 1879 he left Glasgow intending to visit Paris, but settled in London for a time and under the tutelage of John Pettie (1839-93) painted some costume pieces. On returning to Scotland he turned to rustic naturalism inspired by the French painter Jules Bastien-Lepage (1848-84): an example of this phase of his artistic career is shown in Figure 80. In the middle 1880s Guthrie began to concentrate on portrait painting. While oil was Guthrie's normal medium he did produce some works in pastels that were exhibited in the 1890/91 period.

James Guthrie was elected to the Royal Scottish Academy in 1892, becoming President in 1902 and later knighted.

Robert Herdman (1839-88)

Born at Rattray in Perthshire, Robert Herdman was the youngest of the parish minister's four sons. He attended the parish school until he was ten when his father died and his mother moved to St Andrews. At the age of fifteen he enrolled at the University of St Andrews and studied there for the next four years. In 1847 he began art studies at the Trustees' Academy in Edinburgh, later coming under the influence of Robert Scott Lauder. After completing his formal art training Herdman obtained a commission from the Royal Scottish Academy to make copies of works in the Florence galleries; he travelled there in 1855 and spent a year making a number of watercolour copies.

In contrast to many of the other notable Scott Lauder pupils, Robert Herdman remained in Scotland with a residence in Edinburgh. His culture and erudition led to his presidency of the Edinburgh Art Club and vice-presidency of the Society of Antiquaries of Scotland.

Herdman painted in both oil and watercolour. Many of his works are of Scottish historical subjects, but biblical events were also depicted. Single figures and portraits, often of good-looking Scottish peasant girls, were also included in his oeuvre. Examples of his romanticised working girls are illustrated in Figures 45 and 54.

John Lochhead (1866-1921)

Born in Glasgow John Lochhead studied at the Royal Scottish Academy Life School in Edinburgh. He initially painted from Edinburgh, but from 1891 to

1894 was at Craigmill near Stirling where Joseph Denovan Adam had founded a School of Animal Painting in 1887. He then travelled abroad, particularly in Europe, before moving to West Kilbride in Ayrshire where he resided between 1900 and 1916. He retuned to Glasgow at the end of his life and died there.

Lochhead was principally a painter of landscape, but some still lifes and portraits were executed. A small number of pictures of poultry were exhibited. Oil was his main medium, but watercolour was also employed.

William Stewart MacGeorge (1861-1931)

William Stewart MacGeorge was born at Castle Douglas. He received his initial art training at the Royal Institution Art School in Edinburgh. In 1884 he travelled to Antwerp where he studied for two years at the Art Academy under Karl Verlat, principally known for his portrayal of animals. Here he met other Scottish artists including Edward Hornel and William Walls, and subsequently became one of the group of Kirkcudbright painters under the leadership of Hornel. On his return from Belgium one of MacGeorge's favourite motifs was children playing in the sunshine. He also painted scenes arising from the legends and ballads of the Borders, and a number of realistic depictions of rural activities; one of these is illustrated in Figure 47.

Hannah Clarke Preston MacGoun (1867-1913)

Hannah Clarke Preston MacGoun studied at the Edinburgh School of Art and The Royal Scottish Academy Life School. During her artistic life she was based in Edinburgh. Miss MacGoun painted principally in watercolour, but some of her work was executed in oil. Her main subject was children's portraiture, but figures and landscapes were included in her oeuvre. She was a prolific illustrator of children's books.

Robert McGregor (1847-1922)

The family of Robert McGregor came from Dunfermline where his grandfather was a designer of linen damask. His father, also a textile designer, moved to work for an English firm in Bradford where Robert was born. His wish was to become an artist, but he was persuaded to become an engineer. After a short period with an engineering firm he ran away to sea, leaving the ship at Bombay to wander around India. He returned home aged about seventeen and settled down to art studies receiving some instruction from an elderly artist in figure drawing and from his father in design. This was followed by attendance at the Trustees' Academy in Edinburgh and later at the Life School of the Royal Scottish Academy. On completion of his formal training he obtained some work as an illustrator for the publishing firm Nelson. His first painting exhibited at the Royal Scottish Academy was in 1873 when he was aged twenty-six.

McGregor's favoured subjects were rural activities, often set in or around the East Lothian village of East Linton. Children were included in many of his pictures; examples are illustrated in Figures 36, 51 and 58. He made many trips to Brittany where he depicted the shrimpers, mussel gatherers and fishers near the shore.

William Darling McKay (1844-1924)

William Darling McKay was born in the village of Gifford in East Lothian, the son of the parish schoolmaster. After schooling in Gifford he entered the Trustees' Academy in 1860, afterwards continuing his art studies at the Royal Scottish Academy's school. In addition to his painting career McKay acted as the Secretary of the Royal Scottish Academy between 1906 and 1924, having been the Academy's Librarian from 1896. He was the author of *The Scottish School of Painting* published in 1906, and edited with Frank Rinder *The Royal Scottish Academy 1826-1916* which appeared in 1917. He was awarded an honorary LL.D by the University of Edinburgh in 1919.

Many of McKay's paintings are of rural scenes, often with details of agricultural activities, set in his native East Lothian although he did paint in other localities in Scotland and visited Holland, France and Belgium. His unsentimental depiction of countryside activities is seen in Figure 49.

William McTaggart (1835-1910)

William McTaggart was born into a crofting family near Campbeltown in Argyll. After a three-year period as an apprentice to a chemist he left and enrolled at the Trustees Academy in Edinburgh. His teachers included John Ballantyne and Robert Scott Lauder, and he gained a number of prizes as a student.

McTaggart married in 1863 and settled in Fairlie, near Largs and within sight of Arran. He began a work routine of sketching in the open on the coast during the summer months and painting large canvases in oil in the winter. Carnoustie on the east coast and Machrihanish on the west coast were favoured localities for his seascapes. In 1889 he moved to Broomieknowe in Midlothian, remaining there for the remainder of his life. McTaggart continued to paint seascapes in the summer, but now also painted landscapes, including scenes of harvesting. Children often featured in his work; examples are presented in Figures 63, 66, 67, 68 and 70.

William McTaggart painted in both oil and watercolour. He did portraiture in the early part of his career, principally as a means of support, but figures, seascapes and landscapes became his principal subjects.

John McWhirter (1839-1911)

Son of a paper manufacturer John McWhirter was born near Edinburgh. He left his job in a book shop in order to study art, later enrolling at the Trustees Academy where he studied under Robert Scott Lauder. He travelled widely in Europe; his paintings of wild flowers in Norway appealing particularly to John Ruskin. After a period based in Edinburgh McWhirter moved to London in 1869 where he settled and remain there for the rest of his life pursing a successful artistic career. He was a friend of William McTaggart and some joint paintings by them survive (Figure 55).

McWhirter was principally a painter of Scottish landscapes, but also painted scenes in Italy, Switzerland, Austria and France. He used both oil and watercolour, and published popular books on painting.

Charles A. Sellar (1856-1936)

Born in Edinburgh, Charles Sellar obtained a law degree at the University of Edinburgh before engaging in painting. He had a studio at 11 Charlotte Street, Perth and was a member of the committee of the Perthshire Artists' Association between 1921 and 1925.

Sellar painted both in oil and watercolour. His subject matter consisted principally of portraits and landscape, in particular, scenes of Perthshire and fishing villages on the east coast.

Edward Arthur Walton (1860-1929)

Edward Walton was born in Renfrewshire and initially studied art in Dusseldorf. For a few years he attended classes at the Glasgow School of Art and became friendly with James Guthrie. He was one of the group of artists that subsequently became known as the Glasgow Boys. Walton painted at Brig o'Turk and Cockburnspath with the group, later spending a period in London between 1894 and 1904. While in London he travelled regularly to paint in Suffolk.

In the early part of his career Walton concentrated on landscapes; he began to include figures in the scenes, and later took up portraiture. He painted in oil, watercolour and was also a skilled exponent of pastel drawings. An example of one of his watercolours is reproduced in Figure 38.

Edward Walton was elected President of the Royal Scottish Society of Painters in Watercolour in 1914, a position he held until his death.

Illustrations

[1] Sheelin' mussels, Auchmithie, c.1895. Reproduced by kind permission of the Fraser Collection.

[2] View of New Lanark. Watercolour by John Winning, c.1818. Reproduced by kind permission of New Lanark Conservation Trust.

[3] Girl climbing ladder in mine. From *Report of the Children's Employmemt Commission (Mines)*, 1842.

[4] Work in mines in East Scotland. Putting using the 'hutchie' and the 'slype'. From *Report of the Children's Employment Commission (Mines)*, 1842.

[5] Putting using the 'slype'. From *Report of the Children's Employment Commission (Mines)*, 1842.

[6] "How children suffered in factories", Illustration by Robert Cruickshank, 1832. ©Billie Love Historical Collection.

[7] "Love conquered fear". Illustration by Augustre Hervieu for *Michael Armstrong: Factory Boy* by Frances Trollop, London, 1840. ©University of Aberdeen.

[8] "Make haste, young un' or they wont leave a turnip paring for us". Illustration by Augustre Hervieu for *Michael Armstrong: Factory Boy* by Frances Trollop, London, 1840. ©University of Aberdeen.

[9] "A serious gentleman as owns a factory". Illustration by Augustre Hervieu for *Michael Armstrong: Factory Boy* by Frances Trollop, London, 1840. ©University of Aberdeen.

[10] Statue of Robert Owen, Newtown, Powys. Reproduced by kind permission of Grant's Photographics, Newtown, Powys.

[11] Scavengers and piecers at work. From *The History of Cotton Manufacture* by Edward Baines, London, 1835. ©University of Aberdeen.

[12] Jute workers, Dundee, c.1900. ©The Trustees of the National Museums of Scotland.

[13] Spinners, Scotland, 1895. ©Billie Love Historical Collection.

[14] Hugh Cameron, *The Spinning Lesson*. Oil on canvas, 63.5 x 51 cm. Glasgow Museums: Art Gallery and Museum, Kelvingrove.

[15] Hand knitting machine, Hawick, 1889. Reproduced by kind permission of Hawick Museum.

[16] Handloom weaving and draw-boy. Engraving by W. Barr from *Reminiscences of Eighty Years* by John Urie, London 1908.

[17] Children in a rope factory, 1815. ©Billie Love Historical Collection.

[18] Family brick making, 1876. ©Billie Love Historical Collection.

[19] Children carrying clay in a brickyard. From *The Graphic*, Volume 3, 1871.

[20] Cobbler, c.1865. ©Billie Love Historical Collection.

[21] Management and workers, Alexander Hall & Sons, Aberdeen, 1862. Courtesy of Aberdeen Journals Ltd.

[22] Work in an alum factory. From Chemistry, Theoretical, Practical and Analytical, as Applied and Relating to the Arts and Manufactures by Sheridan Muspratt, Glasgow, 1860. ©University of Aberdeen.

[23] Glass making. From *Chemistry, Theoretical, Practical and Analytical, as Applied and Relating to the Arts and Manufactures* by Sheridan Muspratt, Glasgow, 1860. ©University of Aberdeen.

[24] Pottery making. From *Chemistry, Theoretical, Practical and Analytical, as Applied and Relating to the Arts and Manufactures* by Sheridan Muspratt, Glasgow, 1860. ©University of Aberdeen.

[25] Death of two climbing boys in the flue of a chimney. From *The Chimney-Sweeper's Friend and Climbing Boy's Album* by James Montgomery, London, 1824. ©University of Aberdeen.

[26] Widow selling her son to a chimney-sweep. From *The Chimney-Sweeper's Friend and Climbing Boy's Album* by James Montgomery, London, 1824. ©University of Aberdeen.

[27] *Oliver escapes being bound apprentice to the Sweep*. Illustration by George Cruickshank for *Oliver Twist* by Charles Dickens, London, 1862.

[28] Edinburgh street hawkers. From *Child Slaves of Britain* by Robert Sherard, London, 1905.

[29] Lucifer Match Girl. From a daguerreotype by Beard. In *London Labour and the London Poor* by Henry Mayhew, London, 1851.

[30] Charles Sellar, *The Paper Seller*. Watercolour on paper, 30 x 24 cm. Reproduced by kind permission of St Andrews Fine Art.

[31] Two girls binding wood. Date and photographer unknown. Scottish National Portrait Gallery.

[32] Boy Caddies. ©George Washington Wilson Collection, University of Aberdeen.

[33] William Darling McKay, *Golfing on Bruntsfield Links*. Courtesy of Bonhams Picture Library

[34] Young Farmworkers, Perthshire, 1904. ©Trustees of the National Museums of Scotland.

[35] Robert McGregor, *Tending the Family Cow*. Oil on canvas, 43 x 55 cm. Private Collection.

[36] *Herd Boys on Iona*. Engraving of sketch by M. Gavarni in *The London Illustrated News*, Sept. 22, 1849.

[37] Edward Walton, *The Young Shepherd*. Watercolour on paper, 28.5 x 21cm. Aberdeen Art Gallery & Museums Collection.

[38] Thomas Dicksee, *The Little Scarecrow*. Engraving of painting from *The Graphic*, Feb.21, 1857.

[39] Farming family group, Selkirk, c.1900. Courtesy of Clapperton Studios, Selkirk.

[40] John Burr, *A Haymaker*. Oil on canvas, 91.5 x 72 cm. Private Collection.

[41] Lifting potatoes, Fifeshire, c.1900. ©Trustees of the National Museums of Scotland.

[42] Robert McGregor, *The Last of the Potatoes*. Oil on canvas, 61 x 91 cm. Private Collection.

[43] Hugh Cameron, *Gleaners*. Watercolour on paper, 23.5 x 38 cm. Dundee Arts and Heritage. McManus Galleries.

[44] Robert Herdman, *An Arrochar Gleaner*. Oil on canvas, 51.5 x 61 cm. Aberdeen Art Gallery & Museums Collections.

[45] Smithy, Shetlands, c.1905. Reproduced by kind permission of Shetland Museum.

[46] Family at the peats, Loch Fannich, Ross-shire, 1890. Reproduced by kind permission of Mr Colin Campbell.

[47] William Stewart MacGeorge, *A Galloway Peat Moss*. Oil on canvas laid on panel, 81 x 134.5 cm. National Gallery of Scotland.

[48] Hector Chalmers, *The Bark Strippers*. Oil on canvas, 24 x 34 cm. Reproduced by kind permission of St Andrews Fine Art.

[49] William Darling McKay, *Children Playing Outside a Village*. Oil on canvas, 51.5 x 77 cm. Private Collection.

[50] Bringing home firewood, Morar, c1905. ©Trustees of the National Museums of Scotland.

[51] Robert McGregor, *Gathering Winter Fuel*. Oil on canvas, 30.5 x 45.5 cm. Private Collection.

[52] Robert McGregor, *Gathering Driftwood*. Oil on canvas, 48 x 69 cm. Private Collection.

[53] Bringing home bracken. ©Trustees of the National Museums of Scotland.

[54] Robert Herdman, *Young Girl*. Oil on canvas, 43 x 33 cm. Private Collection.

[55] William McTaggart and John MacWhirter, *The Bramble Gatherers*. Oil on canvas, 76 x 51 cm. Reproduced by kind permission of St Andrews Fine Art.

[56] Fisher boys, Newhaven, c.1846. Scottish National Portrait Gallery.

[57] Women and children baiting lines, St Andrews, c.1850. Scottish National Portrait Gallery.

[58] Baiting the lines, Auchmithie, c.1895. Reproduced by kind permission of the Fraser Collection.

[59] Digging for bait, Saltcoats, Ayrshire. Reproduced by kind permission of the North Ayrshire Council Museum Service.

[60] Crew of fishing vessel, Peterhead, c.1860. Reproduced by kind permission of Aberdeenshire Council.

[61] William Marshall Brown, *The Mussel Gatherers*. Oil on canvas, 41 x 61 cm, dated 1900. Private Collection.

[62] William McTaggart, *The Bait Gatherers*. Oil on canvas, 66 x 84 cm, dated 1879. National Gallery of Scotland.

[63] Collecting seaweed, East coast of Scotland, c.1900. Reproduced by kind permission of the Fraser Collection.

[64] William Marshall Brown, *Gathering Kelp*. Oil on canvas, 71.5 x 91 cm. Private Collection.

[65] William McTaggart, *The Fishers Landing*. Oil on canvas, 89 x 134.5 cm. Hunterian Art Gallery, University of Glasgow.

[66] William McTaggart, Fisher Children. Oil on panel, 20.5 x 30.5 cm, dated 1876. Private Collection.

[67] William McTaggart, *The Young Fishers*. Oil on canvas, 72.5 x 108 cm, dated 1876. National Gallery of Scotland.

[68] Robert Noble, *Reddin' the Line*, Oil on board, 23 x 13.5 cm. Reproduced by kind permission of the Rendez-Vous Gallery, Aberdeen

[69] William McTaggart, *The Old Net*. Oil on canvas, 46.5 x 61 cm. Aberdeen Art Gallery & Museums Collections.

[70] William McTaggart, *Going to Sea*. Oil on panel, 46.5 x 39.5 cm. Private Collection.

[71] Babyminding, Renfrewshire, c.1890. Reproduced by kind permission of Greenock Library.

[72] Robert McGregor, *Breakfast Time*. Oil on canvas, 61 x 91.5 cm. Reproduced by kind permission of St Andrews Fine Art.

[73] William Dyce, *A Scene in Arran*. Oil on board, 35.5 x 50.5 cm. Aberdeen Art Gallery & Museums Collections.

[74] Hugh Cameron, *The Little Housewife*. Oil on canvas, 40.5 x 30.5 cm. Dundee Arts and Heritage. McManus Galleries.

[75] Hugh Cameron, *Responsibility*. Oil on canvas, 80.5 x 65.5 cm. Aberdeen Art Gallery & Museums Collections.

[76] William Darling McKay, *Feeding the Poultry*. Oil on canvas, 21.5 x 28.5 cm. Private Collection.

[77] John Lochhead, *In the Farmyard*. Oil on board, 25.5 x 35.5 cm. Reproduced by kind permission of St Andrews Fine Art.

[78] James Guthrie, *The Hind's Daughter*. Oil on canvas, 91.5 x 76 cm. National Gallery of Scotland.

[79] Hannah C. Preston McGoun, *Children at the Well*. Oil on canvas, 37.5 x 27 cm. Private Collection.

[80] Boy carrying pitchers to field workers, c.1905. Reproduced by kind permission of the Buchan Heritage Society.

[81] Thomas Faed, *The Woodcutter's Children*. Oil on panel, 51 x 69 cm. Private Collection.

General Bibliography

Caw, James L., *Scottish Painting Past and Present 1620-1908*, London, 1908 (reprinted Bath, 1975).

Baines, Edward, *History of the Cotton Manufacture in Great Britain*, London, 1835.

Devine, T.M., ed., *Farm Servants and Labour in Lowland Scotland 1770-1914*, Edinburgh, 1984.

Donnachie, Ian, *Owen of New Lanark and New Harmony*, East Linton, 2000.

Gaudie, Enid, *Spinning and Weaving*, Edinburgh, 1995.

Gulvin Clifford, *The Tweedmakers. A History of the Scottish Fancy Woollen Industry 1600-1914*, Newton Abbot, 1973.

Hammond, J.L and Barbara Hammond, *The Town Labourer: 1760-1832*, London, 1917.

Hardie, William R., *Scottish Painting: 1937 to the Present*, London, 1990.

Harris, Paul and Julian Halsby, *The Dictionary of Scottish Painters 1600-1960*, Edinburgh, 1990.

Keeling, Frederic, *Child Labour in the United Kingdom. A Study of the Development and Administration of the Law Relating to the Employment of Children*, London, 1914.

McEwan, Peter J. M., *Dictionary of Scottish Art and Architecture*, Woodbridge, 1994.

Martin, Angus, *Fishing and Whaling*, Edinburgh, 1995.

Montgomery, James, *The Chimney-Sweeper's Friend and Climbing-Boy's Album*, London, 1824.

Sherard, Robert H., *The Child-Slaves of Britain*, London, 1905.

Strange, K.H., *Climbing Boys: A Study of Sweeps' Apprentices 1773-1875*, London, 1982.

Thomson, Alistair G., *The Paper Industry in Scotland 1590-1861*, Edinburgh, 1974.

Urie, John, *Reminiscences of Eighty Years*, London, 1908.

Index